I0410412

Coral Reef Coloring Book

30 Hand Drawn, Doodle and Folk Art Style Coral Reef and Marine Life Adult Coloring Pages

ISBN-13: 978-1539565499
ISBN-10: 1539565491

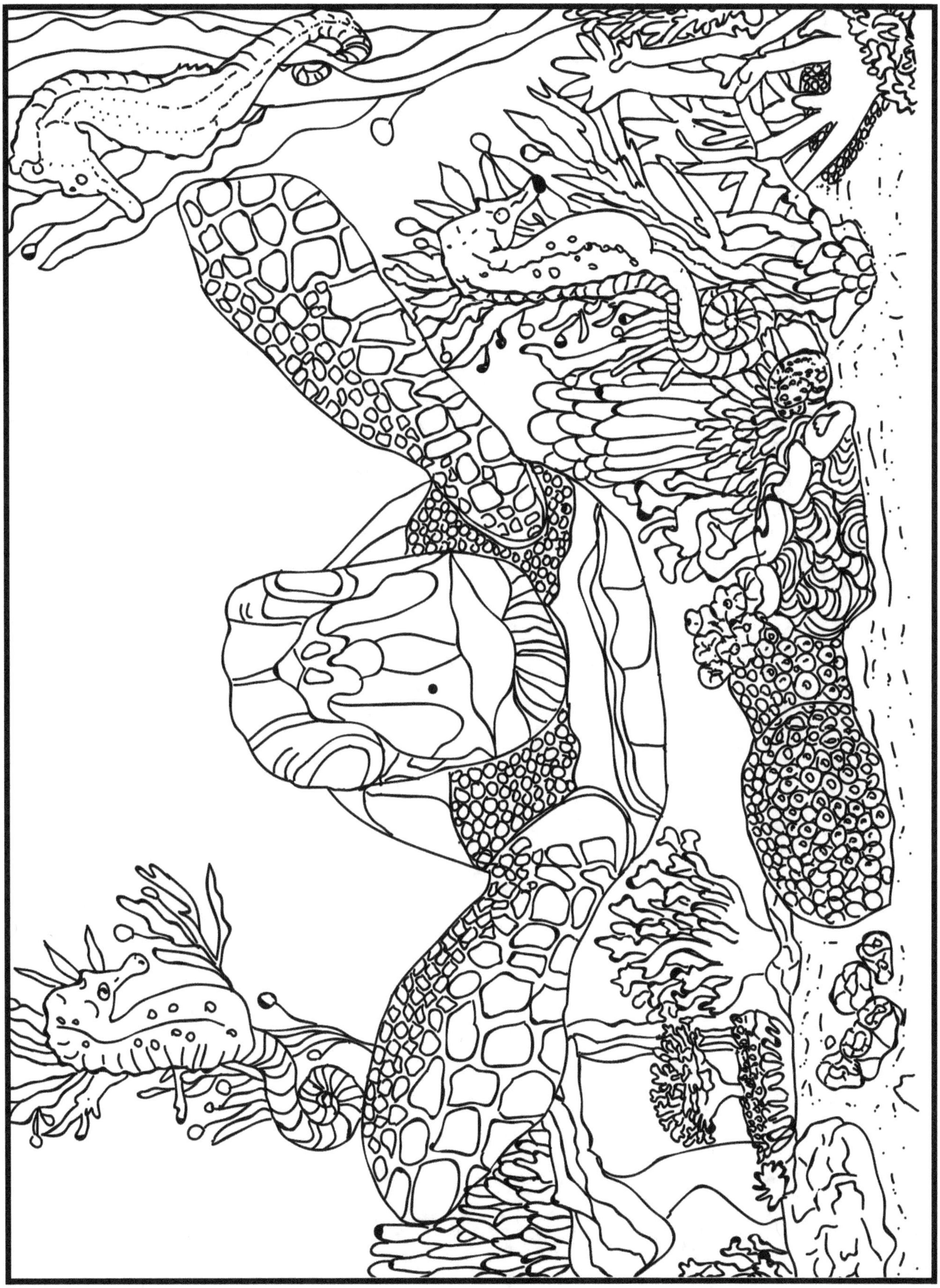

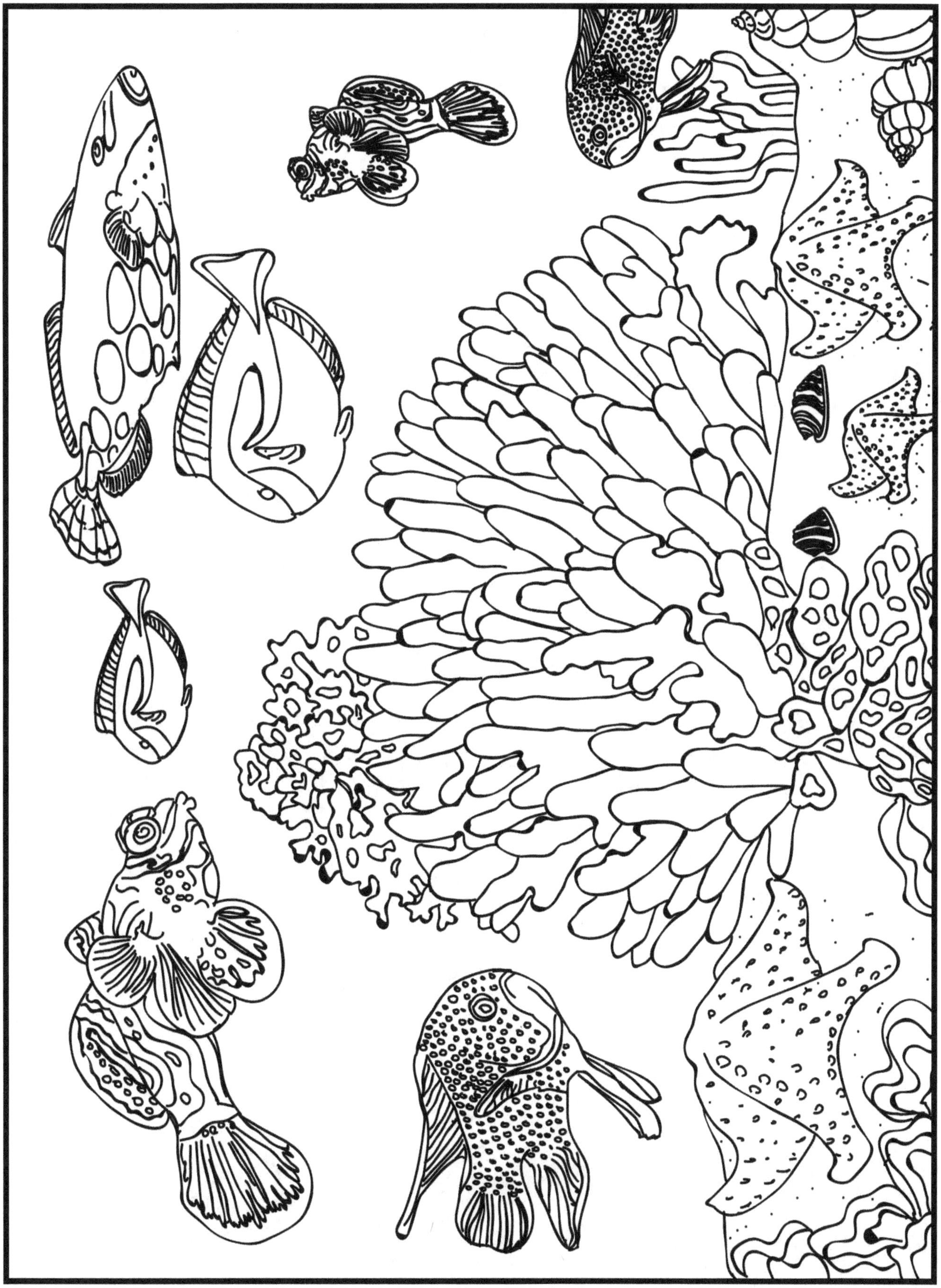

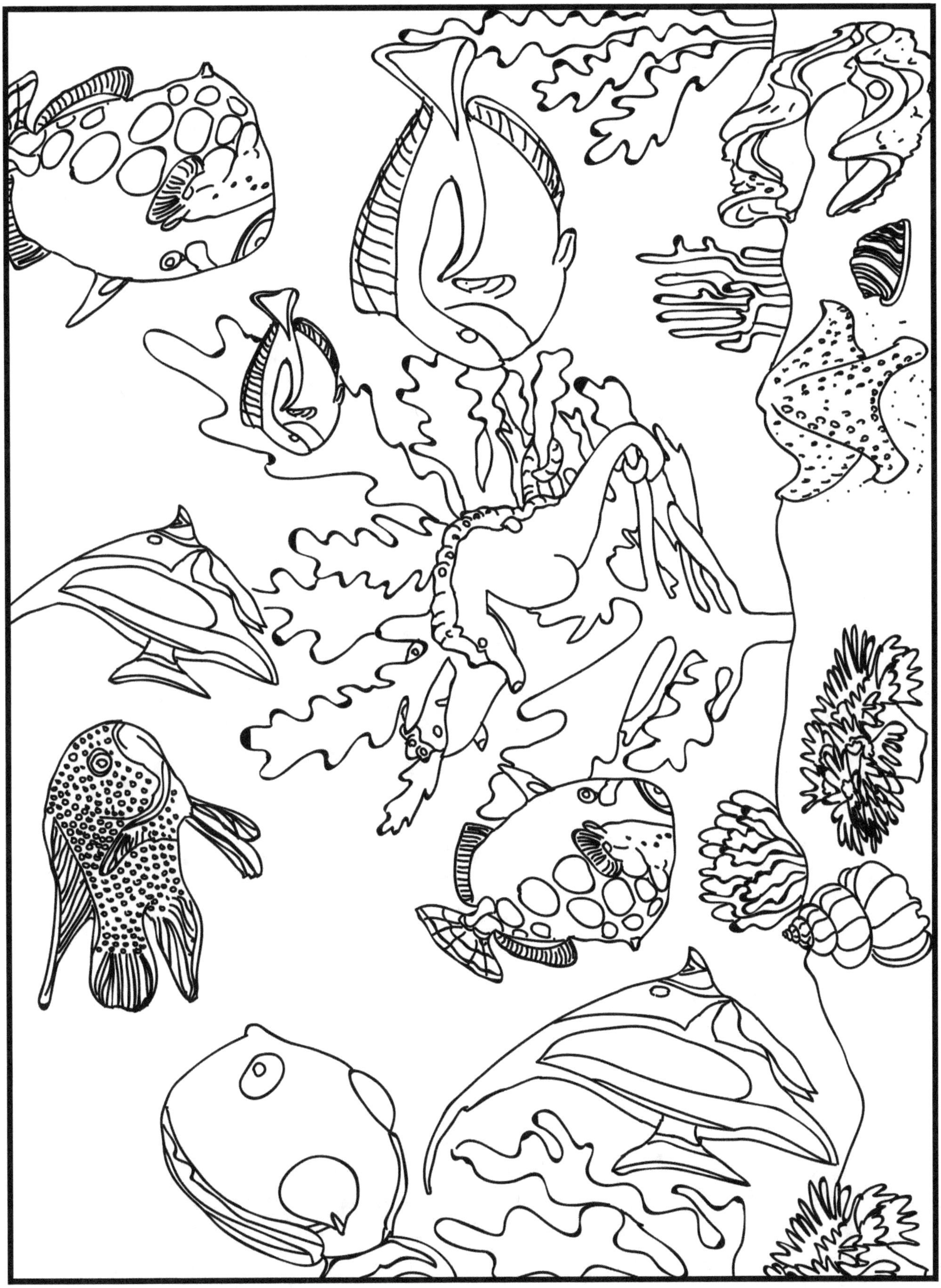

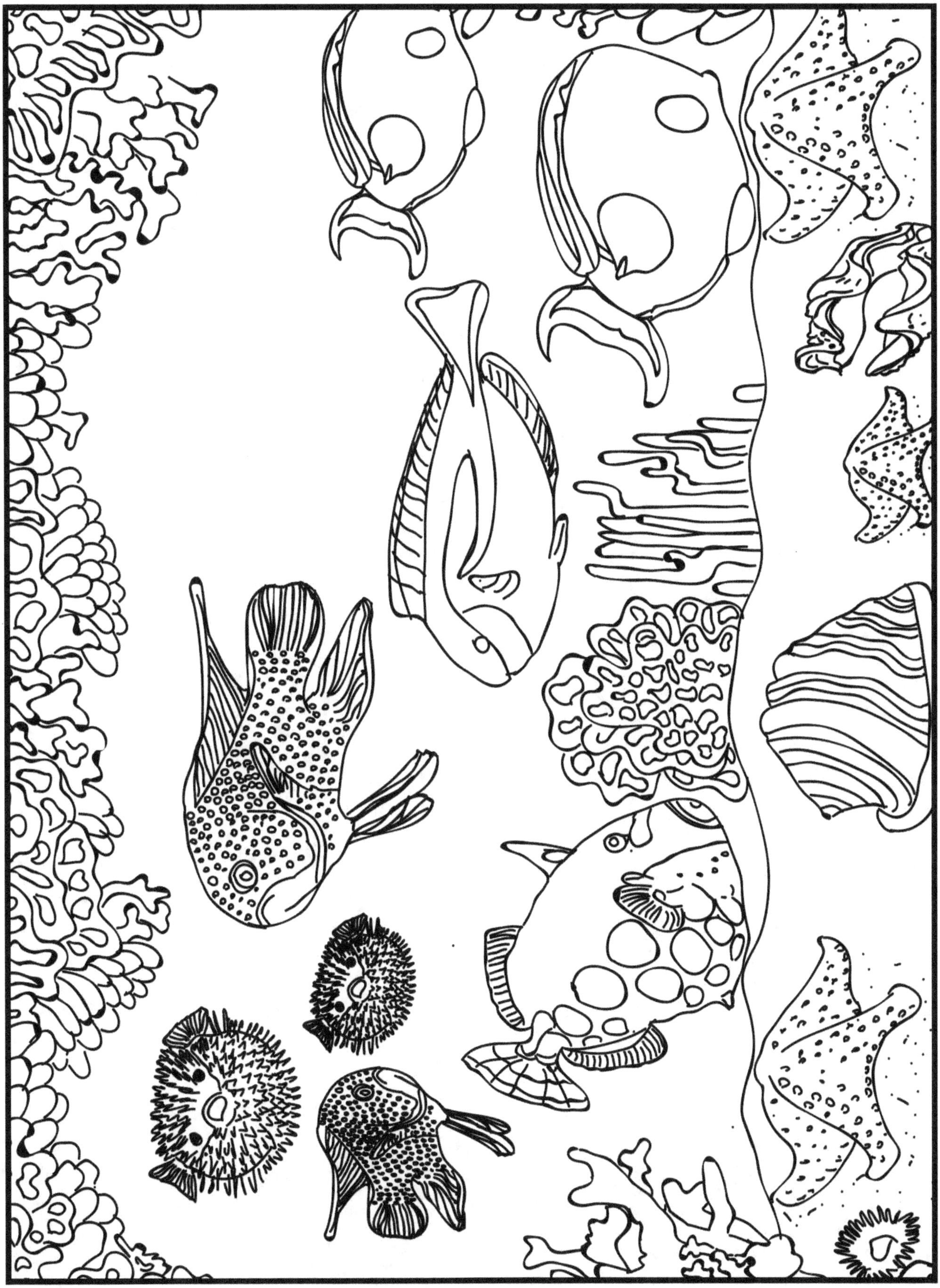

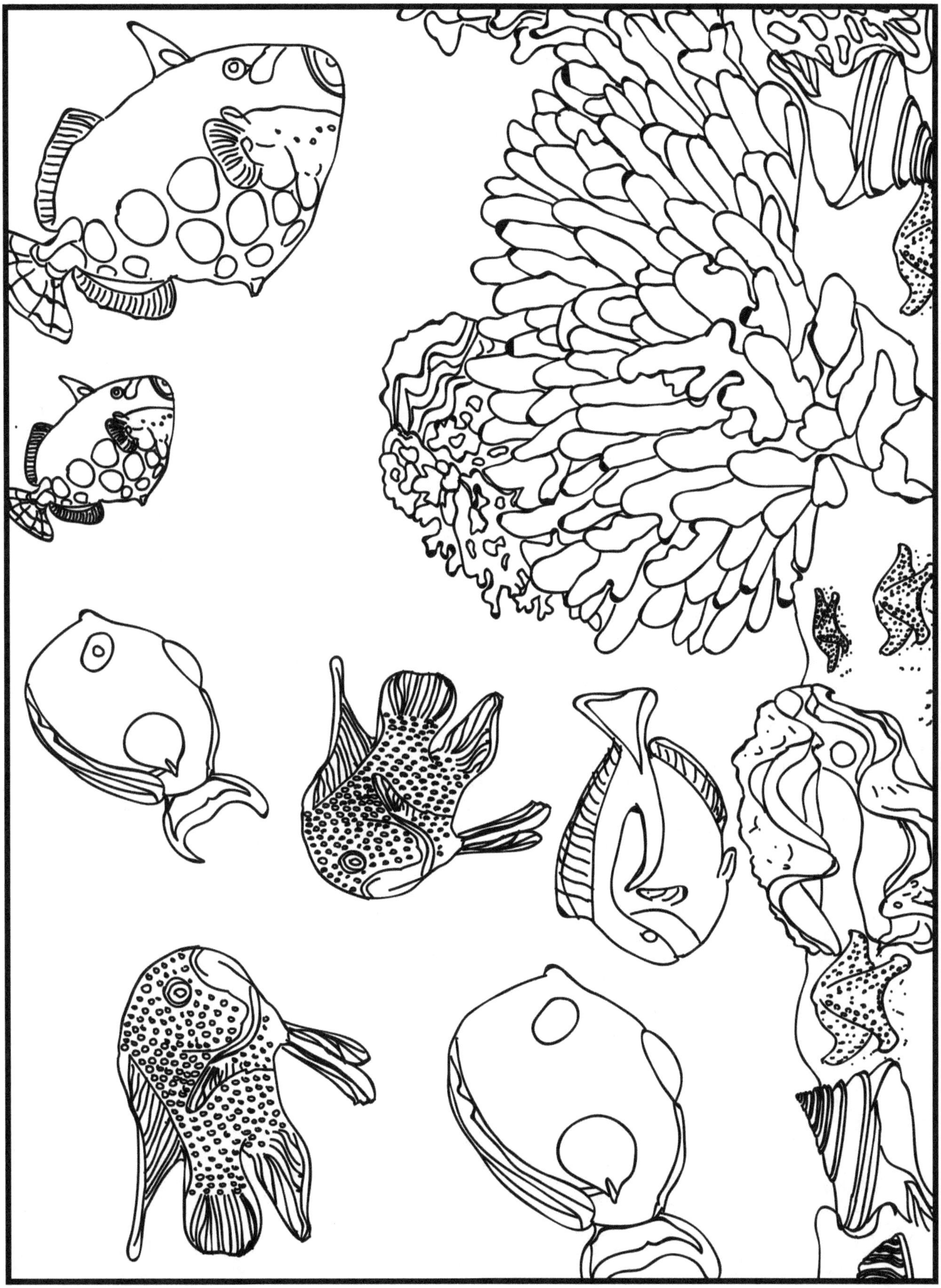

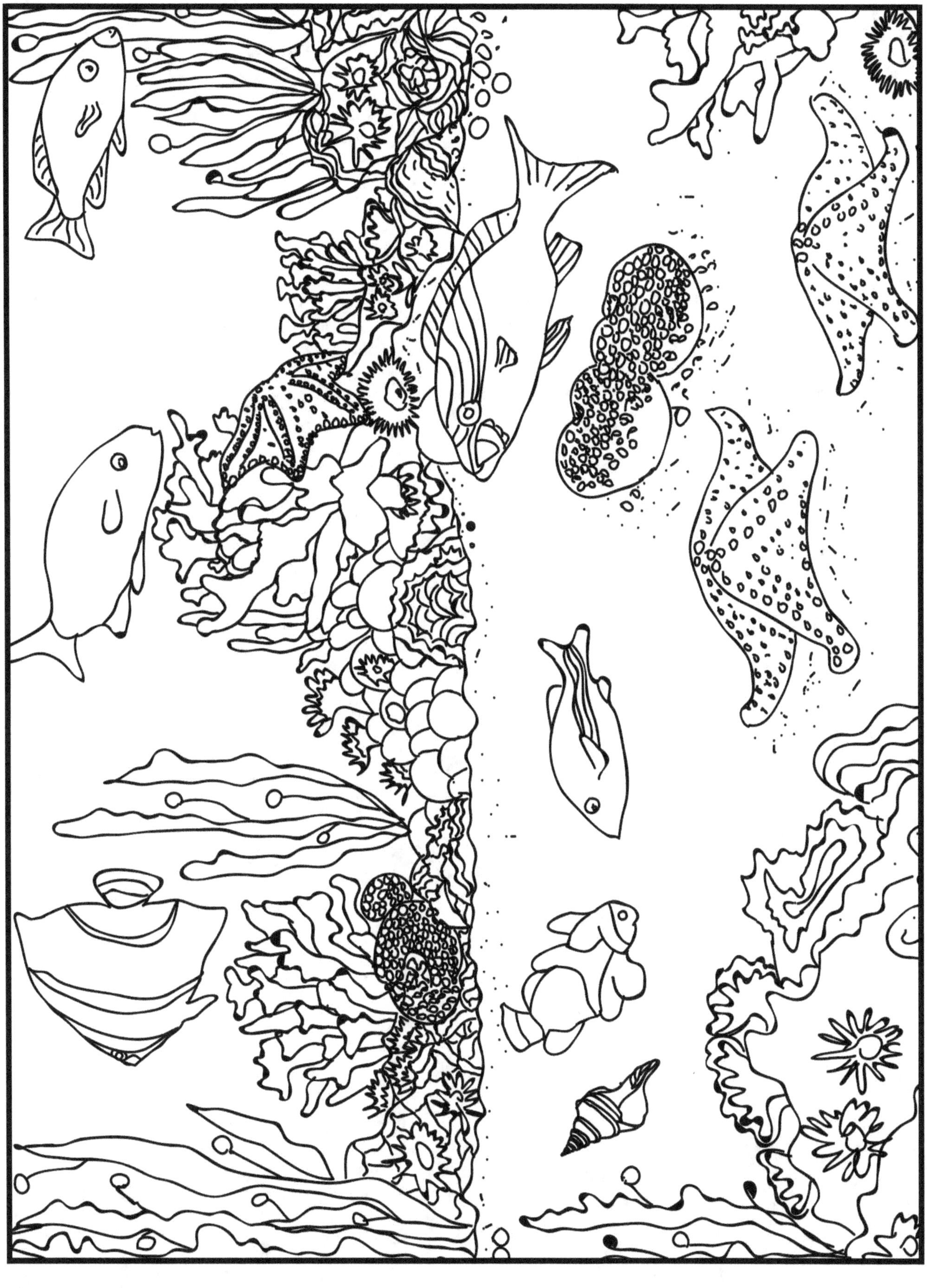

www.ingramcontent.com/pod-product-compliance
Lightning Source LLC
Chambersburg PA
CBHW081859280526
45789CB00007B/2760
* 9 7 8 1 5 3 9 5 6 5 4 9 9 *